Then
England
Education
⟶ Photograpshy

Village Camera

by

MISS PINNELL

with the help of

THE CHILDREN OF
SAPPERTON SCHOOL

ALAN SUTTON

First published in the United Kingdom in 1990 by
Alan Sutton Publishing Ltd · Phoenix Mill · Far Thrupp · Stroud · Gloucestershire

First published in the United States of America in 1991 by
Alan Sutton Publishing Inc · Wolfeboro Falls · NH03896–0848

British Library Cataloguing in Publication Data

Pinnell, Miss
Village camera
1. Gloucestershire. Sapperton, history
I. Title   II. Children of Sapperton School
942.417

ISBN 0–86299–791–7

Library of Congress Cataloging-in-Publication Data

Pinnell, Miss
Village camera / by Miss Pinnell with the help of the children of Sapperton School
p.   cm.
ISBN 0–86299–791–7
1. Sapperton (England) – Social life and customs – Pictorial Works
2. Sapperton (England) – Description – Views
3. Villages – England – Sapperton – Pictorial Works
I. Sapperton School   II. Title
DA690.S235P55   1991
942.4'17– –dc20

Jacket pictures:

Children of Sapperton School with a *c.* 1885 camera from the collection of
the late Jack Porter (Pat Pinnelll). Sidney and Lucy Barnsley with their
children Edward and Grace. Photograph courtesy of Mrs Tania Barnsley.

Design and typesetting by
Alan Sutton Publishing Limited.
Colour origination by
Yeo Valley Graphic Reproductions, Wells.
Printed in Italy by
S.p.A New Interlitho, Milan.

FOREWORD
by HRH The Duke of York

BUCKINGHAM PALACE

Every day history is made but all too often our past is forgotten. Before the advent of the camera we have had to rely on drawings and books to establish much of our heritage.

Photography is an enjoyable way of illustrating our memories. It is a hobby which has given me, personally, a great deal of enjoyment and satisfaction.

It is sad to see so many old photographs being forgotten and often destroyed. With this in mind I am delighted that the children of Sapperton School have put together a collection of photographs depicting the history of their village.

I hope "Village Camera" acts as an incentive to other communities to follow their example.

INTRODUCTION
by Lord Lichfield

Photography is a comparative newcomer to the visual arts. Although we do not know the precise date of the first photograph, we do know that it was little more than 150 years ago. In this short time it has also become one of the most widely used visual records and even more recently has spawned the media of film, television and video. The relative mechanical simplicity of taking a standard photograph has given an extraordinarily wide range of people a means of keeping a visual record of individuals, places and events – both public and personal. The children of Sapperton have discovered for themselves how even a cardboard box can be turned into a crude pinhole camera; today almost every tourist travels armed with a camera of some sort.

In the early days, exposure times were long and the instantaneous facility of photography had to wait for the development of faster acting films and improved optics. All the same, even early photographs could be taken in minutes, whereas a painting might take hours. Now we have the phenomenon of a still image of a bird in flight or an athlete on the track, as well as some of the most sophisticated photographic techniques.

What *Village Camera* shows is the remarkable versatility of photography and photographers in those early days. The camera has given people a marvellous opportunity for creativity – to compose a picture and record a moment, a gesture, an expression; and to do so for an audience of one or a private family album. What Miss Pinnell and the children of Sapperton School have discovered is that, in time, a community builds up a remarkable record of itself without being aware of it. Many individuals with their own independent collection of photographic moments recorded in old sepia prints and tucked into envelopes, corners or attics, never realize that gathered, sorted and compared, they can form a unique and evocative jigsaw of interrelated images. A child in one portrait photograph reappears as an adult in another and as an onlooker to the event in a third; his daughter marries and enters the albums of another family and so the elements start to weave themselves into a fascinating and widening tapestry of a community.

Of course photography has also developed into a highly respected art form, often commanding international recognition in its individual character style and excellence; but the value of those old, sometimes fading, forerunners of the art has taken longer to establish itself and there are still many images which end up on a bonfire or thrown out. My hope is that in their demonstration of this exciting photographic heritage, the children of Sapperton School will encourage others to preserve and value these unique images of our past.

Lichfield

The photographic history of Sapperton village is recorded here in 'Village Camera," an account of country people brought to life by the advent of the camera.

When our first book "Village Heritage" was published, it received much publicity. The television, radio and Press carried news of its success nationwide.

Memories were stirred...

Letters began to arrive at tiny Sapperton C. of E. School. Former pupils, ex-Sappertonians and village friends wrote to congratulate us and to reminisce about village days long gone.

Many enclosed faded photographs; canal boatmen, railway workers and agricultural labourers rub shoulders with country gentlemen, and our excitement mounted as we studied these and realised what a wealth of detail and information lay before our eager eyes.

PUBLISHERS' NOTE

Village Camera is presented as it was written. The book is in manuscript, not typescript; the old photographs are reproduced by kind permission of their owners and the majority of the modern prints are Miss Pinnell's own; the story itself is unbroken by editorial interruptions. From time to time, however, these boxes in the margins will go behind the scenes to show some of the many people, museums and trips which helped to supply the answers and create a suitable setting for the children. It is hoped that these will act as an inspiration and a pointer to others, who wish to trace their own local history.

I

Village Heritage – The book which started the flow of correspondence.

The children needed to write numerous letters to forge the links which have enabled this project to be completed.

Some of the photographs were taken before the turn of the century. We studied them closely, researching costumes, occupations and locations, bringing our rural history to life.

Exactly where were they taken? What did these places look like now?

Many pictures were accompanied by anecdotes, enriching our knowledge of Victorian and Edwardian village life, and our interest increased even more.

We replied to each correspondent and further material followed as friendships were built up.

Publicity about *Village Heritage* produced letters from various parts of the world: some from those who remembered the village of their childhood and others who knew and loved the area from past holidays.

These two plate cameras, *c.* 1885, part of the collection of the late Jack Porter, were of particular interest to the children, as cameras like these would have been used to take many of the sepia prints which they collected.

1898

While letters arrived from far away recalling ancestral links with our neighbourhood others much nearer at hand also produced photographs of those days long ago.

Farmers found boxes in attics; school governors recalled old pictures hanging on walls; pupils searched through grandparents postcard albums, and all added to our ever increasing collection.

As we looked at these faded prints our fascination grew. What were they like, these often unsmiling people who stared at us from these old photographs?

They were our past... our photographic heritage!

3

The postman became a regular visitor to the school bringing a steady stream of correspondence. Each letter required an answer, and the children were kept busy replying and requesting permission to use the most interesting photographs which were often included with the letters.

When we had worked on "Village Heritage" we had noticed so much was recorded of the rich, the powerful and the talented.
  But here, in these faded prints are captured memories of the ordinary folk who walked our ways and peopled our valley, frozen by the camera lens for all time.

Sapperton Village.

Sadly, many prints are destroyed as owners die and houses are cleared. Cherished memories go up in smoke!
  If only we could collect a representative selection of these pictures we would feel that we were preserving another part of our heritage for future generations.

4

It was seeing a bonfire like this that prompted Miss Pinnell and the children of Sapperton School to begin this project. Unfortunately, some people regard old photographs as 'junk', often burning or dumping what others would consider to be important documents.

As we looked at these people from our past we tried to practice empathy.

We tried to imagine what they were really like. We tried to get "inside their skins".

To do this we visited the places they trod and wore the clothes they might have worn. Sometimes we handled the tools they once held.

The children really enjoyed dressing up in period costumes and trying to understand and experience the lives of those people whose history they were discovering. Many locals did not have running water or bathrooms and Joanna was able to acquaint herself with the difficulties involved in bathing in a tin bath in front of the fire; with the cooperation of her baby brother!

At Daneway.
8.5.17.

Some pictures depict hardship and sadness. Some have a pathos not so obviously apparent.

This view of Daneway in 1917 was taken by young Gerald Drummond who lived at The Chantry, Bisley.

At the turn of the century, aged 10, he was given his first camera. He toured the neighbourhood recording what he saw.

The World War came and he went off to fight for his country. Five months after taking this picture he went to France, never to return. His broken-hearted family locked his room and never opened it again. The house and contents were sold around 1926 to the Churchill family. They opened the sealed room and found all his albums, labelled as he left them in 1917. A family member allowed Stanley Gardiner, a local photographic historian, to copy them and he shared this information with us.

A photograph of The Chantry, Bisley from Juliet Shipman.

These are some of our earliest photographs, probably taken around 1870.

Moira Gobey, our school cook, found this one of her Great-Great-Grandfather Oakley who lived in a cottage near the top of Cowcombe Hill in 1860.

Thomas Fisher, the village centenarian, was listed as a pauper, aged 84, on the 1851 census, dating this picture about 1867. It was given to the late Norman

Jewson, father of one of our school governors, around 1930.
  Above we see Esther, born 1788 and Jonas Workman, born 1795, both listed as paupers in the 1871 census. Miss Jewson donated it also.

The children used the 1871 census of Sapperton to find out the ages and other details of Esther and Jonas Workman.

Fox Talbot was experimenting with photography around 1840 and by 1861 there were 3000 professional photographers in Britain.

Ten years earlier there had only been 50. We have not been lucky enough to come across any of these very early prints though we like to imagine that when the first trains steamed through Sapperton Tunnel on Whit-Monday 1845, Fox Talbot, knowing Brunel, could have travelled down from his home at Lacock Abbey in Wiltshire to witness his friend's triumph with the opening of the line.

The viaduct opposite, at Frampton Mansell, was one of nine along the valley. In 1845, when the first trains rattled over it, they had put their faith in one made of wood.

8

The junior class did experiments to find out about light, pinholes and reversed images to help them understand the difficulties facing early photographers.

In the 150th G.W.R. Jubilee Year during
August 1985, King George V, a "Castle" class
engine came our way. Never before had
such a "heavy" been allowed on this route.

c. 1860

Some time later, so the railway records tell us, these wooden
viaducts were encased in brickwork.
The old picture of an unidentified viaduct near Stroud shows
the wooden strength of these structures.

1912

The people of this area have had close connections with the railway from its early days and as we researched our photographs we discovered two who lost their lives going about their duties.

On Sept. 14th 1861, this gentleman, Richard Charles Hooper was born.

His father, Richard Hooper of Frampton Mansell was a porter at Stroud Station and was fatally injured there in January 1862.

Richard Charles was the youngest of five children that widowed Eliza was left to bring up, his grand-daughter, Mary Godfrey of Basildon informed us.

When young Richard Charles was aged 8 he went to work on a farm 2 miles from home, leaving school probably to supplement the family income. He continued to educate himself with copybooks.

He began his police career in Cheltenham, June 1881, later transferring to Gloucester and Cardiff. (He was sent to Bristol for a Royal Visit and said Queen Victoria was so tiny she had to stand on a footstool.)

Stroud G.W.R. Station
about 1862

Another family with strong links with the G.W.R were the Carringtons. Thomas Carrington, born July 13th 1851 and his wife Susannah, born March 31, 1853, lived in Sapperton and had six children, John William 1878, Edith Fanny* 1880, Francis Richard 1881, Ethel Rosina 1883, Jessie Eleanor 1887, and Albert Edward 1889.

The names, dates and details on these two pages came from the family Bible of Audrey Ricks of Churchdown. The pictures came from her grandmother's* Victorian photograph album.

Jessie Carrington is shown on this picture of Sapperton School around 1898.

12

In this picture, taken at the same time as the one opposite, we see the youngest Carrington, Albert Edward, (usually known as Bob).

His father, Thomas, was employed by the Great Western Railway from 1872 – 1917.

1894   A younger Albert Edward

We traced Thomas, the father of this family, on the 1871 census. He was an unmarried under shepherd then, aged 19 years.

The 1851 census showed his father and mother, Richard and Sarah, living here so Thomas must have been born after the census was taken.

Old photographs came from all sorts of sources.
Our mobile school librarian, Audrey Ricks, provided us with Albert and John, seen here, while Stan Gardiner, a local photographic historian, found Thomas

1906

We saw an older Albert, aged about seventeen, at his garden gate, opposite where the Village Hall would be built in 1912,

and discovered his older brothers John (above) and Francis were also G. W. R. men.

Our story is taken a stage further with Thomas, Albert's father who worked in the Sapperton Signal Box from 1874-1917. This picture also shows the old wide rail track.

Stanley Gardiner, local historian and author, helped with the school's researches and provided some of the photographs.

Then a letter arrived....

A correspondent, Nora Annesley of Egham, Surrey, wrote:
" In those days there were only two political parties,
Conservative and Liberal. The people were divided.
Mrs. Carrington (pictured left) worked for the Liberal
Cause by hanging out a yellow flag and made
her views known.

In 1906 the Liberal, Mr. Essex, was returned to
Parliament. She made much of this and teased
known Conservatives when she saw them.

Late one dark night they painted her door
blue (the Conservative colour). To put people off
the real culprits, they dribbled the paint to
various houses, including the Police Station
and the Rectory.

The dog didn't bark and the family knew nothing of this until
the morning. There was much talk and speculation as to who had done
it. I remember asking my father if he had made the paint. He replied,
"No, but I know who did!" Villages were not quiet little places where
nothing happened; such incidents were talked about for weeks. "

In 1915 the family moved from the house below the Bell, opposite the Village Hall, to live at Chalford Hill.

Chalford Signalman's Sad End.

FOUND DEAD ON THE LINE.

At an early hour on Tuesday morning the body of Thomas Carrington, of Chalford Hill, near Stroud, was found in the four-foot way on the up line of the short tunnel at Sapperton. The deceased, who was 66 years of age, was a signaller in the employ of the Great Western Railway Co., and during Monday had been assisting Mr. Fred Stafford, of Cowcombe Farm, Chalford, in harvesting. He left Mr. Stafford's home at 9.30 p.m., and was last seen alive a quarter of an hour later by a man named James Phelps, of Frampton Mansell. He was then going in the direction of the Sapperton signal box, where he had been employed for many years and where he was due to arrive on duty at 11 p.m. He did not reach the box, and enquiry was made and the line searched with the sad result stated. The body was removed to Chalford Station, to await the inquest.

Mr. R. H. Smith (deputy coroner) held the inquest at the Red Lion Inn yesterday. Mr. Gunter was chosen foreman of the jury. Mr. A. H. G. Heelas represented the family on the instructions of the National Union of Railway Servants, and Mr. E. T. Evans, inspector of Gloucester, was present on behalf of the Railway Company.

Frederick Richard Carrington, son of the deceased, a shunter in the employ of the G.W.R. and living at Gloucester, said his father had been in the employ of the Company for 45 years and for 43 years of that period he had been attached to the Sapperton Signal Box. He enjoyed good health.

James Phelps, carter, in the employ of Mr. Fred Stafford, said he was engaged all day on Monday with the deceased and they parted at 9.40, about a mile and a quarter from the Sapperton signal box. He was quite sober.

Frederick William Wheatley, engine driver, of Brimscombe, said he went up the line twice with the banker engine, and Thomas Cobb, the signalman, reported that Carrington had not been on duty and asked him to look out. He did so with his flare lamp and found deceased in the four-foot way. He was quite dead and the body was cold. There was a fracture at the base of the skull and the deceased was lying with his arms spread open with his head in the direction of Cirencester. There was a bundle of food some little distance away, and in his witness's opinion Carrington was knocked down by an engine as he was proceeding along the line in the direction of the signal box. He took it that Carrington was walking in the four foot way because that was the easier. The ballast in the six-foot way rendered walking more difficult.

Inspector Ernest Thomas Evans said the deceased had no right to be walking on the line. There were very definite rules prohibiting the servants of the Company doing so. His way to the signal box was by the road and there was no need for him to cross the metals at all. By going the line way Carrington would shorten his journey by about 10 minutes' walk.

Replying to the Coroner, Mr. Evans thought that deceased might have been taken ill and fallen on the line and on recovering from a stupor was struck by a train as he was rising. There was a wound on his forehead.

The Coroner: Or he may have felt tired and fallen to sleep by the side of the line as he had ample time to get to the box for duty.

Mr. Evans: Yes, but I think the probabilities are that he stumbled and fell and injured himself so much that he had to rest some time before attempting to resume his walk, or he may have been rendered unconscious by the fall.

P.c. Henry Wiggins said he examined the body and he had formed the conclusion that the deceased was knocked down by a train from behind as he was walking in the four-foot way to his work.

The jury returned a verdict of accidental death and expressed sympathy with the family, Mr. Wiltshire remarking that a more devoted husband or a better father could not be.

Mr. Heelas suitably acknowledged these remarks and the enquiry closed.

In this cutting from the local paper, Sept. 1917, and found among the possessions of Edith Carrington, we can read the details of the tragic death of Thomas Carrington, aged 66. PC. Henry Wiggins, the Sapperton policeman at the time, examined the body.

The school plays host to senior citizens, who join the children for lunch. They have a store of memories which they often share with the children and some, like Mrs Roberts, have provided old photographs which they have treasured for many years.

P. C. Henry Wiggins, known as a stern disciplinarian, can be seen (extreme left) in this picture of Frampton & Sapperton United A.F.C. 1919-20. The rest of the back row from the left are Vines, A.W. Cox, G. Harrison (Goalie), E Goodfield (Capt), B. Baxter, —?
Middle row from the left: S. Vines, M. Tuck, C. Ractliffe, Front row left, R. Radcliffe, C. Hanks (Mascot H. Hanks), P. Watts, E. Roberts and H. Ratcliffe.

The late Arthur Roberts, pictured
here as a young soldier, used to recount
his meeting with P. C. Wiggins on
the road from Frampton Mansell to
Sapperton about 1910.
The P. C. asked the then young boy why
he was coming to visit Sapperton.
Young Arthur gave some innocent
reason, only to receive a sharp rap
on the head.
"What's that for, Mr. Wiggins?" he
tearfully asked.
"That's for all the mischief you
are just THINKING of doing, lad."
came the stern reply.

But let us return to our RAILWAY theme. This picture was already hanging on the wall when Mr. Procter, one of our school governors, moved into his home in Frampton Mansell.

As the house is only a stone's throw from the big viaduct and the railway line runs along the bottom of his garden we can guess that they are railway gangers of the same 1912 - 1915 period as the following picture.

Mr. Procter says some earlier occupants of his home were the Selby family who worked for the G.W.R. Mr. Procter was told this tale by them.

"Their daughter was in service at a big house in London and she used the train to travel home whenever she had time off...

"The nearest station to Frampton Mansell was Chalford. The train had to travel along the young lady's garden boundary before it reached Chalford a couple of miles further on.

She came to a friendly arrangement with the engine drivers whereby they slowed the train down as they passed her garden, thus enabling her to gently toss her hand luggage into her own garden as the train chugged slowly past. This saved her having a heavy burden to carry when she alighted at Chalford and walked back through the lanes to Frampton Mansell."

This picture shows gangers at the mouth of Sapperton Railway Tunnel 1912-1915 (2nd right is Fred Whiting and seated is one of the Carrington boys who does look like the man third from the right in the back row of Mr. Procter's picture.)

So the photographs continue to interweave with the history of our village ....

Photograph and information – Stan Gardiner.

... and with each letter a fuller understanding of our past emerged.
In another epistle, Nora Annesley, born 1900 in Sapperton wrote, "My mother used to tell me, when she was young, (c. 1880?) a special train used to run from Swindon into Hailey Woods (the line from Swindon to Gloucester and South Wales ran through this way) and the people from the Swindon railway works got off the train and spent the day gathering nuts. At a given time they all boarded the train and returned home.

Early in October <u>we</u> were given two days holiday from Sapperton School to gather hazel nuts, (around 1906 - 1910). Mothers would prepare a meal for us to take, cakes, sandwiches, cold tea and lemonade, as aunts and cousins accompanied us.
We carried crooks made of bent sticks to reach the tall branches. The keepers and woodmen told us where the best nuts could be found."

This card of the Sapperton kitchen of Norman and Mary Jewson which was sent to William Simmonds, Oakridge, on 2.7.1927, and given us by local postcard collector, Howard Beard, shows what a kitchen looked like in those days.

We sent to Gloucester Library for copies of the Census Returns for 1851 and 1871. We found them a great help in dating photographs and checking families. These are families with Railway wage earners.

FRAMPTON 1851

Name:		Age:	Occupation:
Thomas Gibbons		24	Rail Police
Sarah	"	19	Wife
Louisa	"	9 months	
William Aldworth		27	Rail Police
Maria	"	27	Wife
George Hunt		31	Rail. Police
Ann	"	32	Wife
Emma	"	6	Scholar
George	"	4	Scholar
Edward	"	2	
Robert Meecham		26	Rail. Lab.
Ann	"	24	Wife
Joseph	"	6	Scholar
Maria	"	5	
Mary	"	1	

FRAMPTON 1871

Eliza Hooper		38	Widow
Charles	"	16	Porter GWR
Rebecca	"	11	
Richard	"	9	Silk Winder
William Drinkwater		27	Gateman
Eliza	"	27	Wife at Crossing

FRAMPTON (CONT) 1871

Luke Gardener		39	Rail. Lab
Elizabeth	"	41	Wife
Louisa	"	12	Silk Winder
Emma	"	11	Silk Winder
Mary	"	9	Scholar
Ellen	"	2	
Thomas Gibbons		45	R. Police
Sarah	"	34	Dame school T.
George	"	15	Undergroom
Charles	"	7	Scholar
Francis	"	5	Scholar
Arthur	"	1	
Job Townsend		61	Rail. Lab
Fanny	"	57	Silk Picker
George	"	34	Masons Lab.

SAPPERTON 1851

William Meecham		29	Rail. Lab.
Eliza	"	28	Wife
Sarah Ann	"	8	
William	"	6	
Jemima	"	5	
Robert	"	3	
Frederick	"	10 months	

SAPPERTON (CONT) 1851

John Hutton		27	Rail. Policeman
Sarah	"	29	Wife
Emily Jane	"	4	
Sarah Harrison		66	Mother in Law
Henry Jones		24	Rail. Lab
Harriet Jones		32	Wife
James	"	1	
Henry Gibbons		62	Railway Contr.
Hannah	"	42	Wife
Edwin	"	16	Rail. Lab.
Jane	"	15	
Fanny	"	10	
Anne	"	8,	Henry 6

SAPPERTON 1871

Samuel Pope		58	Rail. Switchman
Ann	"	57	Wife
William Hooper		40	Rail. Lab
Deborah	"	39	Wife
George	"	10	Agr. Lab.
Frank	"	8	Scholar
Mary Ann	"	3	
Alice	"	1	
John Gardener		47	Rail. Lab
Hester	"	49	Wife
George	"	20	Rail. Lab.

22

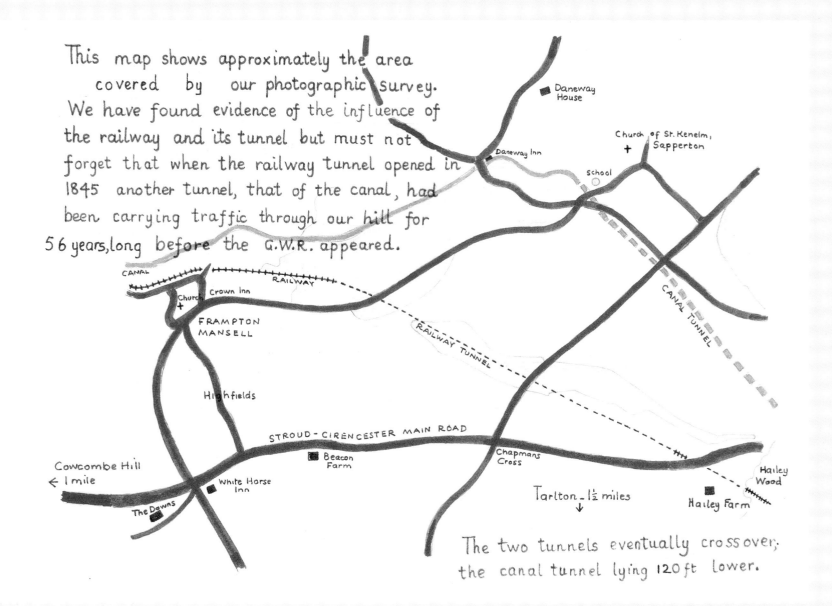

This map shows approximately the area
covered by our photographic survey.
We have found evidence of the influence of
the railway and its tunnel but must not
forget that when the railway tunnel opened in
1845 another tunnel, that of the canal, had
been carrying traffic through our hill for
56 years, long before the G.W.R. appeared.

CANAL

RAILWAY

Church
Crown Inn

FRAMPTON
MANSELL

Highfields

Daneway
House

Church of St. Kenelm,
Sapperton

Daneway Inn

School

CANAL TUNNEL

RAILWAY TUNNEL

STROUD - CIRENCESTER MAIN ROAD

Cowcombe Hill
← 1 mile

Beacon
Farm

White Horse
Inn

The Downs

Chapmans
Cross

Tarlton - 1½ miles
↓

Hailey
Wood

Hailey Farm

The two tunnels eventually crossover;
the canal tunnel lying 120 ft lower.

One of the earliest Canal tales:

Long, long ago, in 1788 just before ships travelled through our tunnel, an old man lived in a cottage beside the Dareway Inn, which was then called the Bricklayers Arms.

This old man, whose name was Cainey, was walking along the towpath of the new canal, near his home, when he saw several rich gentlemen. One of them spoke to poor, old Cainey.

BY CHANCE I DID ROVE

❧

NORMAN JEWSON

One of the school governors, Miss Jewson, gave the children this book, *By Chance I Did Rove*, by her father, Norman Jewson. It gives a detailed account of life in Sapperton between 1907 and 1918. Norman Jewson was closely associated with Ernest Gimson and the Barnsleys.

When we first heard the story of "Cainey's Gold" we said, "If only cameras had been invented then ... "

"Do you know who I am, Old man?" said the rich gentleman. Cainey shook his head. The gentleman took a guinea from his pocket and told Cainey to take a good look at the head on one side of it.

"Now look at me", commanded the gentleman. Cainey suddenly guessed who stood before him. "Lor bless us, its the King," he cried and sure enough it was. The King let him keep the Spade guinea and his family treasured it for years. The King had come to see our marvellous tunnel.

What an idyllic journey of serenity and beauty must have been experienced by those early boatmen as they travelled up the Chalford Valley to the bustling, busy Daneway Basin! But not an easy passage to be sure; the 28 locks coming up from Stroud made sure of that.

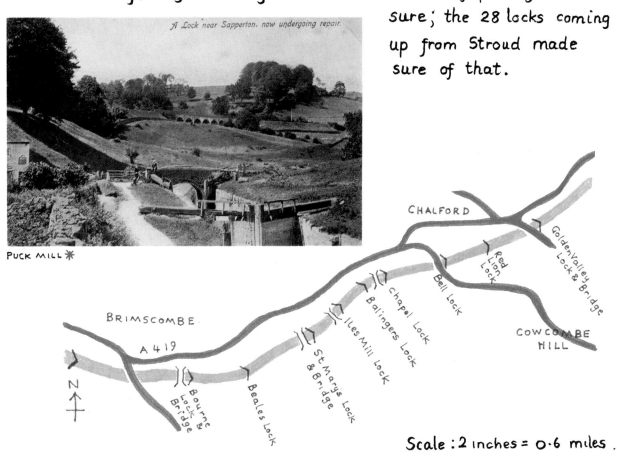

A Lock near Sapperton, now undergoing repair.

PUCK MILL ✳

CHALFORD

Golden Valley Lock & Bridge

Red Lion Lock

Bell Lock

Chapel Lock

Balingers Lock

Iles Mill Lock

St Marys Lock & Bridge

COWCOMBE HILL

BRIMSCOMBE

A 419

Bourne Lock & Bridge

Beales Lock

N ↑

Scale : 2 inches = 0·6 miles.

The boatmen must have witnessed a rural England before imminent mechanical changes altered a way of life that had carried on for centuries, and we started to build up a picture of a small part from the photographs.

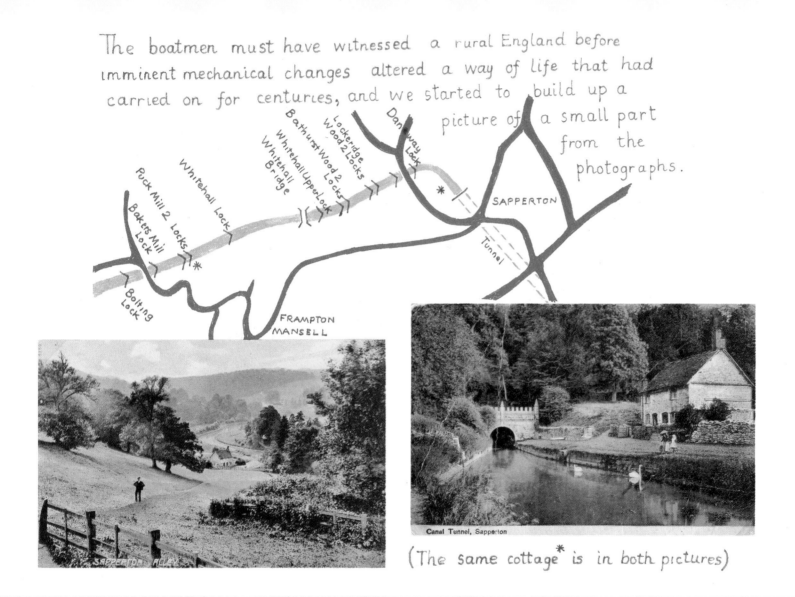

Puck Mill 2 Locks
Bakers Mill Lock
Bolting Lock
Whitehall Lock
Whitehall Bridge
Whitehall Upper Lock
Bathurst Wood 2 Locks
Lockeridge Wood 2 Locks
Dan way Lock
SAPPERTON
Tunnel
FRAMPTON MANSELL

SAPPERTON ALLEY

Canal Tunnel, Sapperton

(The same cottage* is in both pictures)

27

1920

As the boatmen worked their way towards the Summit they found refreshments at the many inns beside the locks. At Puck Mill Double Lock the host of the Oak Inn, Samuel Elliot, stands waiting with his wife, Emily.

Around 1922 when trade from canal boats dropped, the Oak Inn closed and became Puck Mill Farm instead.

Parents like Mrs Robbins, who has many local connections as well as a personal interest in old photographs and other documents, which she willingly shared with the children in the course of this project, provide a vital link between the community and the school.

At the turn of the century Daneway waited, locks ready and pounds filled with water. The old boat waited too; however, the daily supply of drinking water still had to be fetched from the spring.

The children experienced the hard work involved in fetching and carrying water when they were given this old yoke.

We believe this picture, given by Miss Gobey, shows a major County Council reconstruction at Puck Mill lock in the early 1900s, but the canal's heyday had passed.

This interesting and detailed photograph shows the same area and was taken around 1902-1904. We particularly noted the centre group of men working to reline the bed of the canal with clay, an activity known as "puddling". This restoration cost approximately £30,000.

CLAY PUDDLING

The children discovered in their study of canal building that the most important ingredient of an efficient canal is water. The canal's water must be of sufficient depth, usually 5 feet, to allow boats to float freely. Water must not be allowed to leak away as it is often hard to replace.

Canals need to be watertight, holding in the water. The ditch that forms the bottom of the canal has to be lined to make it watertight. Usually, from the earliest canals, clay has been used to form this lining. The clay has to be specially mixed up so that it has no lumps. It is then spread on the bottom and beaten flat.

This is known as "puddling". Water was often lost because the clay dried out and cracked before the water flooded in. When the water leaked out the canal was closed for long periods and boats were stranded.

A puddling gang at work around 1904.

Stanley Gardiner, who had these two pictures in his collection, said that Annie Hyett, slightly left of centre, born 1874, from Weston, Bath, and visiting relatives in nearby Chalford, little realised how she would be immortalised when asked to pose by a photographer as she walked by the canal at Sapperton.

After years of restoration the first boat passed the Summit on March 3rd 1904 and when this picture was taken, in 1906, the canal committee hoped trade would return to the Daneway Basin.

Picture from Miss Leach via S. Gardiner.

In 1909 Lord St. Aldwyn called the canal a 'white elephant' but parties still enjoyed a trip through the tunnel to Tunnel House. This is a Brimscombe group of friends in 1912.

Living beside a canal was a bit like living beside a motorway – everything passes but nothing stops, at any rate, not for very long! Only the name Thomas Jones features in the 1871 Census to tell of a boatman's roots. To find out more of our waterborne heritage we visited the Waterways Museum at Gloucester.

Anyone tracing the past of their own area should speak to people like Moira, Sapperton's school cook, and her mother who have spent their whole lives in one place seldom, if ever, moving house.

Here a Sapperton crew take over the narrowboat "Northwich". Such boats had to be legged through Sapperton Tunnel while the towing horse would be walked up the hill towards Coates.

TUNNEL MOUTH SAPPERTON

We started to see how photographs can chronicle change.

This picture, taken around 1900, is one of the most photographed views on the canal. In 1934-1960 when Moira Gobey, our school cook lived there, it was such a popular spot for walking, that she and her mother provided outdoor afternoon teas. Moira's grandfather, who lived here from 1898 until 1947 was responsible for the maintenance of the canal for many miles.   In the 1851 census it housed the family of Eleanor Meecham, (5 adults, one schoolgirl and a lodger who was a mason's labourer) Now sadly it is only a ruin.

37

Victorian and Edwardian ladies loved to send and collect postcards as a hobby. The two below, though not of known local views, were purchased and received within the area in October 1905 and show a nostalgia for rural life even then.

This was a prolific time for local view cards. We received most of those opposite from an ex-pupil who was at school when they were taken. She is the grand-daughter of John Blowen, headmaster here from 1853 – 1886.

SAPPERTON, GLOS.

TAUNT & CO. 1740

The Bell, Sapperton.

Sapperton School & Village.

She particularly remembers the man in front of the school picture. He was Raymond Midwinter, the cowman employed by Mr. Chamberlain of Manor Farm. He lived in a small cottage on the left of the path which rises between the posts opposite to the school.

39

We felt we were very fortunate to make contact with Mrs. Nora Annesley. It was when she saw the above photograph of Sapperton School of 1906 in the "Daily Mail" that she first wrote to us. She told us that she was the little girl, third child from the left, in the second row up. She was born Nora Harrison at "The Mount", near St. Kenelm's Church, Sapperton on November 5th 1900, but now lives in Surrey. She is just brimming over with stories of those far off days and delighted to share those memories with us. In the larger picture she is 17 years old.

Articles in national newspapers concerning *Village Heritage*, produced many letters from correspondents such as Nora Annesley, now aged ninety and living in Egham, Surrey. She proved to have a particularly vivid store of memories and information about her early years in Sapperton and was able to give today's children detailed accounts of school life at the turn of the century.

In her early letters she told us more about the school picture. She vividly recalled the death of Miss Bertha Martin, headmistress, who is standing on the right of the picture. As her coffin was carried out from the School House, the schoolchildren who had been previously assembled in the school yard, watched and sang her favourite hymn "Praise to the holiest in the height". Miss Martin was not buried in Sapperton but taken by motor hearse to her family home in Clifton, Bristol.

She also recalls happier times. Because Mr. Midwinter's cottage had very little garden, his wife was allowed to hang her washing on the Village Green. As the school playground was small and our grassy banks at the back were the boys' gardens, the older children were allowed on the Green to play cricket. When the wind was blowing the washing well it was considered to be an even greater sport to try to throw the cricket ball into the billowing legs of Mrs. Midwinters knickers!

Her grandfather, Mr. Blowen, trained a yew-tree in the garden of School House so that it was like a room inside, and she was delighted to hear that David, the boy who lives in School House now, still uses it as it was intended.

Mrs Annesley, who is 90, has such a keen memory of those days at the beginning of the century; she can even tell us that on the classroom wall hung a large map of the world showing the British Empire and a wall chart telling the story of the Gloucestershire Regiment, its battles and its honours. We asked her to tell us about a typical school day around 1906.

A Day at School in Edwardian Times.

My name is Nora Annesley, I was a little girl at Sapperton C-of-E School in the early 1900's, this is how I remember our day was spent.

The bell was rung at 8.50 a.m., if fine we stood in lines to march into school, if wet we hung our cloaks and went into class. Girls and infants hung cloaks in one porch and boys in the other.

Prayers and a hymn were sung, the sliding doors closed for the infants separate lessons. Until 9.45 a.m., Scripture, reading from the Bible, learning new hymns and Catechism, then the register was called.

Arithmetic was always the first lesson of the day, followed by English, History, Geography, Reading until 12 o'clock, with a break for playtime at 10.45 a.m. Grace was sung at 12 o'clock, after the Reverend Cropper came in, then we had to curtsey saying, each time, "Good-morning Sir, Good-morning Miss, Good-morning Teacher".

At 1.20 p.m. we returned for afternoon lessons Grace was sung, and every day, tables 2 X 1 to 12 X 12 = 144 chanted in a sing-song way and then tables of measurement, liquids etc., these were usually found on the backs of Exercise Books. The remainder of the afternoon was spent learning poetry, painting and drawing for the boys, the girls sewing pinafores, knitting socks, making samplers in cross-stich etc. with a break at 2.45 for afternoon playtime.

Nora attended the school prizegiving day in July 1990, travelling from Egham to join the children.

A small cupboard on the wall contained reading books which were allowed on Friday afternoons for those who had done good work during the week.

The School was heated by pipes round the walls, in winter the mornings were cold and by afternoon too hot. We sat in desks for four children. The Infants consisted of Baby Class, Second Class Infants and Standard I, Standards II to V in the "big" room. The girls went to school in red cloaks provided by Countess Bathurst she also gave the boys navy blue jerseys.

Inspectors came occassionally, the Diocesan Inspector once a year, if answered well, we were given a Certificate, a holiday was given in the afternoon.

To help us understand Nora's description of school life in the early 1900s we went to Gloucester Folk Museum where it was quite an eye-opener for the children of today to experience the rigid lessons and strict discipline of a Victorian classroom for an hour. Although very different from school today, with proper preparation how they enjoyed it, completely accepting the master's despotic rule!

Studying the two Census Returns revealed a large number of paupers. In 1851 there were 17 of them and 12 in 1871, (dictionary definition: a poor person, especially one who is supported by the public) before Lloyd George introduced pensions in 1909.

We wondered how they existed in the valley. Mrs. Annesley gave us a clue when she wrote of her Victorian headmaster grandfather, John Blowen, who taught in a classroom similar to the one opposite.

"On Sundays the Blowen children were sent to take dinners to poor widows; this before they had their own meal.

"He (Mr. Blowen) was sorry for children who had to leave school at an early age to work on the farms and in the large houses. Two evenings in the week, after school and when the boys came home from work, he walked to Frampton Mansell to continue with their lessons. These lessons were held in a shed lent by a farmer, the boys paying one penny each for candles to light the room."

It would appear that those who had the means felt that they were obliged to help the less fortunate whenever possible.

Picture from Mrs. J. Clements/c.1901

A well known village character, the Reverend Hugh Cropper is standing at the left of this 1915 photograph. He led the village spiritually and socially from 1884 for 34 years. He is best remembered by the young for his generous gift of fireworks every Nov. 5th. Maurice Tibbles, himself a well-known photographer of T.V. nature films, sent this picture.

His mother, who now lives in Cirencester, is in the front row, as are Dorothy and Etheldrida Whiting of Tunnel Mouth Cottage. Matthew Tuck is 2nd from the right in the back row.

The children of Sapperton and Frampton Mansell have attended the school in Sapperton since it was built in 1848 by Earl Bathurst.

They have, over the years, built up a tradition for entertaining school plays, apparent here in this pre-1914 photograph of their production "Green Broom."

46

Sir Charles and Lady Darwin (who we believe came from Painswick) were great friends of the Gimsons of Sapperton. Lady Darwin became involved with the school and wrote some plays especially for the Sapperton school children.

These were based on old songs, one of which was "Green Broom". The Darwins came to see the plays performed in the new Village Hall, which had been built in 1912 as a gift to the village by Lady Bathurst.

Mrs. Gimson (who is mentioned again later) made the dresses for the plays and the children often went to her house, "The Leasowes" to rehearse.

This view looks towards the Village Hall, centre; the right-hand building is the old Police Station where P.C. Wiggins dealt out justice before, during and after World War I. This 1925 picture was provided by Miss Jewson.

Gloucester Record Office was an invaluable source of information. Like all record offices, it holds many local documents, photographs, maps and records, all of which provide the researcher with an excellent starting point.

Travel was very difficult for most people in the early years of the century and only a lucky few found their way to the sea-side. Jessica Carrington became an infant teacher at Chalford Hill School.

Here she (on the left) and her two friends Flora (centre) and Ada Smith (right) display their matching swimming costumes at Weston-super-Mare about 1918.

Chalford Tabernacle had close links with our area, thanks to the Clark family at the Downs Farm.

Here is Jessica again, we think soon after World War I, as Great Britain (centre) in a chapel tableau based on "Our Empire".

Both pictures from Doreen Gardiner, Ebley.

As the search for prints widened and news of the school project spread, more people turned out their cupboards: Miss Gardiner of Ebley found her mother's photographs in a shoebox.

48

A Baby Show was once held in the field beside the Bell Inn, Sapperton and this 1907 picture, given by Ken and Freda Drewett, recording the event, is one of our favourite scenes.

Thus we were particularly pleased to hear from Godfrey Simmonds, now of Wimborne, who was the first prize winner. He said there was so much animosity among the losing mothers (they came to blows!) that it was decided never to hold such a competition again.

Many people were able to send information as well as photographs, helping to build up a detailed picture of life at that time. Godfrey Simmonds wrote to reveal that he was the winner of the Sapperton Baby Show of 1907 and enclosed the photograph taken of him to mark the occasion.

It was after the Boer War, 1899 – 1902, that Lieut. General Sir Robert Baden-Powell became impressed with Scouting as a training for good citizens. In 1908 boys began forming groups of Boy Scouts.

The picture on the right shows P. C. Wiggins as Scoutmaster with the 1908 Sapperton Troop, possibly one of the earliest formed.

Matthew Tuck and his brother Arthur are seated at the front. This photograph, taken at camp with their bell tent, was sent to us by Matthew's daughter, Mrs. Pat Whittington of Castle Douglas.

The Sapperton Morris Men, in the early 20s, gave pleasure to many, often dancing in front of Sapperton Church.

Here, in Cirencester Park, we see from the left: Frank Whiting, Jack Harrison, Alf Cobb, Reg. Whiting, Frank Gardiner's leg and E. Cobb.

Farming families in the vicinity had often farmed the same land for generations and could fill in background details to many questions. Farmer Rex Tuck was able to identify his father, Arthur, and his Uncle Matthew in the front row of this photograph.

This survey is a social history in photographs.
It spans approximately one hundred years. It is about people ; how, when and where they lived. But it is <u>by</u> people, too.
It has only been possible because people have preserved pictures and mementoes of the past and have been willing to share them with us.
So it was a great joy to have met 'squirrels' in our researches ... to meet people who store away old pictures, documents and memories of days gone by, really treasuring the past.
We met two such collectors in Ken and Freda Drewett of Frampton Mansell. Freda spent a happy childhood at the Downs Farm and willingly provided us with many photographs and information about a family who influenced their community for over half a century.

Andrew Drewett arrived home with a large box of prints, saved from a bonfire when Downs Farm was being cleared following the death of Florence Clark.

Collectors, such as Ken and Freda Drewett, have a fund of information and memorabilia which is valuable to those researching the recent history of their own locality.

21.7.1907

THE DOWNS GARDEN PARTY

In the early part of the century, the Downs Garden Parties were great social attractions, but the story really begins a few years earlier.

In 1886, when they were much younger, this couple moved from Chalford to the Downs Farm, near Frampton Mansell.
Charles and Alice Clark were staunch Baptists and supporters of the Liberal Party.

EAST GLOUCESTERSHIRE GOSPEL TEMPERANCE UNION.

I, the undersigned, do PLEDGE my Word and Honour, GOD HELPING ME, to abstain from ALL intoxicating Liquors as beverages – wine, beer and cider included – and that I will, by all honourable means, encourage others to abstain.

DATE.	NAME.	AGE.	PROFESSION.	RESIDENCE.
April 23rd 1884	George Arnold X witness C. E. Clark.	32		Frampton Mansell
	Thomas Whiting	44		"
	Louisa Whiting	19		"
	Mary Bateman	15		"
	Bessie Phelps	17		"
	Mary Vines	16		
	Ellen Vines	14		
	Emily Pymer	14		
	Annie Hill	10		
	Alfred Fryman	11		
	Sarah Bateman	12		
	Jane Vines	11		
	George Phelps	13		
	Joseph Vines	9		
	Joseph W. Vines	10		

Peter Watts 'passes' the Crown Inn, F. Mansell. c. 1910

As we can see from this page, the family encouraged others to follow their own strict moral code.

Charles was a Deacon of Chalford Tabernacle and Alice was a teacher at the Sunday School. We know from the census that the farm they bought had, in 1871, supported 16 working men and 10 boys, plus 2 Servants.

Soon after he bought the Downs Farm, Charles Clark had the stock valued. These prices of a hundred years ago would surely appeal to the farmer of today.

We could see from the census just how many farms were in our area:

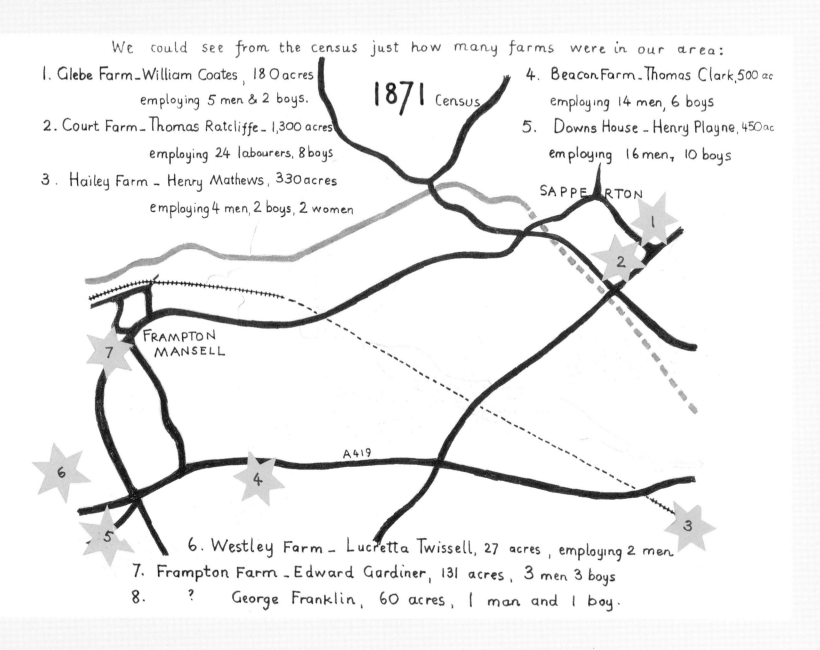

1. Glebe Farm — William Coates, 180 acres employing 5 men & 2 boys.

2. Court Farm — Thomas Ratcliffe — 1,300 acres employing 24 labourers, 8 boys

3. Hailey Farm — Henry Mathews, 330 acres employing 4 men, 2 boys, 2 women

1871 Census

4. Beacon Farm — Thomas Clark, 500 ac employing 14 men, 6 boys

5. Downs House — Henry Playne, 450 ac employing 16 men, 10 boys

SAPPERTON

FRAMPTON MANSELL

A 419

6. Westley Farm — Lucretta Twissell, 27 acres, employing 2 men

7. Frampton Farm — Edward Gardiner, 131 acres, 3 men 3 boys

8. ? George Franklin, 60 acres, 1 man and 1 boy.

Florence

c. 1908

Elizabeth

Harry

In 1890 Eva Clark was born, in 1893 Florence, and then, in 1901 Elizabeth. On the far right is a young friend of the family, Harry Whiting.

At a time when most girls did not expect to pursue academic goals the Clark girls achieved a great deal.

Eva, born 1890, attended Stroud High School (Locking Hill) and read Medicine at Edinburgh University. Then she went to India as a mission doctor.

For Bessie, born 1901, Stroud High School was followed by marriage. One of her daughters, Dr. Elizabeth Marsh, followed Eva's footsteps.

Florrie, born 1893, followed her sister's schooling, then trained as a midwife at Manchester, returning home to deliver many local babies.

c.1925

To the young girls growing up, life at the Downs must have seemed idyllic, but farm life was a hard life for many.

When we studied our 1871 census we could see that most boys and some girls could expect their first job to be in some way connected with agriculture, often from the early age of eight.

Carter Hope poses with a favoured horse at the Downs. He can be seen in the smaller picture harvesting. Reaping machines had been introduced in 1860, before that scythes and sickles were used needing many more men to bring in the harvest.

(Rebecca's dad and Scott's mum let us borrow their animals.)

Shepherds and grooms earned more than most farmworkers because they had greater responsibilities. Boys got between 1s 6d and 2s 6d each week. These are some of the young boys who left school to work on farms, from the 1871 census.

(S = Sapperton, F.M.= Frampton Mansell.)

(S) Charles King, 12 years

(S) Thomas Arkill, 10

(S) Thomas Gardiner, 10

(S) William Cobb, 10

(S) Samuel Saunders, 8

(F.M.) Frederick Whiting, 12

(F.M.) Edward Whiting, 9

(F.M.) William Bidmead, 12

(F.M) Elijah Jones, 10

(F.M.) Arthur Jones, 9

(F.M.) James Bidmead, 10

Paul and Adam found how hard the work
was at Beacon Farm. Around 1840 agricultural
labourers earned about 7s - 8s a week.
The seemingly small wages of the boys
really helped poor families.

The cost of living was low. Cottage rents were about 1 shilling a week.
Most cottagers kept a pig or chickens and skim-milk was very cheap.
At harvest time women and children gleaned but as
reaping machines developed they left less corn for the
gleaners so the housewife lost her free bags of grain.

The attic at Beacon Farm revealed a
treasure house of old photographs, early
postcards and other discarded items.

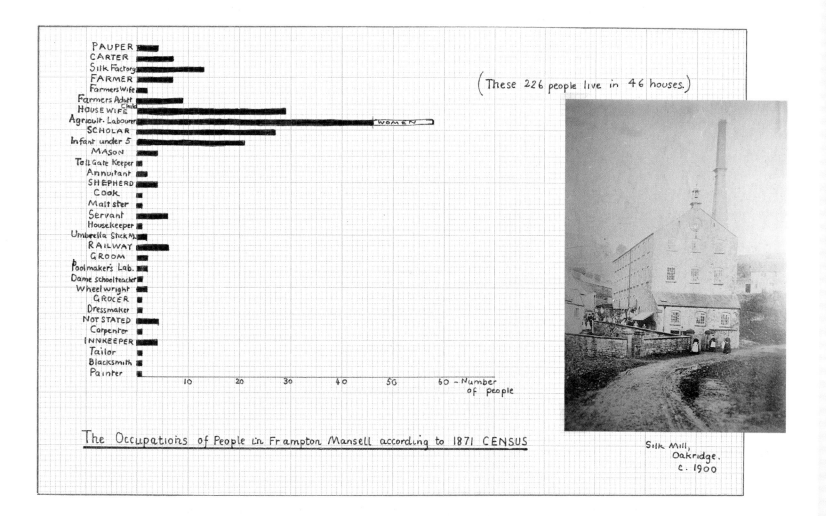

(These 226 people live in 46 houses.)

PAUPER
CARTER
Silk Factory
FARMER
Farmers Wife
Farmers Adult Child
HOUSE WIFE
Agricult. Labourer — WOMEN
SCHOLAR
Infant under 5
MASON
Toll Gate Keeper
Annuitant
SHEPHERD
Cook
Malt ster
Servant
Housekeeper
Umbrella Stick M.
RAILWAY
GROOM
Poolmaker's Lab.
Dame schoolteacher
Wheelwright
GROCER
Dressmaker
Not STATED
Carpenter
INNKEEPER
Tailor
Blacksmith
Painter

10   20   30   40   50   60 - Number
                                    of people

The Occupations of People in Frampton Mansell according to 1871 CENSUS

Silk Mill,
Oakridge.
c. 1900

In a predominantly agricultural area there were other well known families. We talked to the late Ruth Philpotts, who was able to tell us more about life at that time and found splendid pictures for us to show how things were beginning to change...

Here we see the farming family of Henry and Eliza Ractliffe, (Ruth's grandparents) celebrating their Golden Wedding. Their son Sidney (standing far right) and his wife Agnes (seated far right), Ruth's parents, were later to have links with two farms in our area and two just outside it.

Henry Ractliffe, born 1821, lived at Tarlton Farm just south of our area. This picture, taken in 1911, is on the occasion of his 90th birthday and shows all his 10 children and their 8 spouses. Far right, standing, is Henry Clark of Beacon Farm (who was the brother of Charles at the Downs Farm.) Seated far right is his wife who was Lucinda Ractliffe. After Henry Clark's death, Sidney and Agnes (standing 2nd and 3rd left) took over the running of Beacon Farm.

Sidney and Agnes arrived at Beacon Farm, on the main Stroud-Cirencester road, early in the 1920s. They came by pony and trap but later had one of the first 'bull-nosed' Morris cars in the area. The very early steam tractor is an International Harvester 8-16 Junior.

Stanley, Cyril, Philip, Ruth

Philip

Lucy

These are some of the children of Sidney and Agnes. Walter, their sixth child, to whom we spoke, is not shown. He said Philip, with his air-gun, is standing beside a Lister pump, which on bath nights was used to pump cold well-water up to the bathroom. Then the youngest child would take up one bucket of hot water from the copper and bathe. The second youngest carried up another bucket of hot water, bathed and was followed by the rest doing the same, adding each time, ending with Mum and Dad! No loitering allowed!

Gradually more machinery came into use on local farms, replacing many traditional farming methods. The family took many ploughing prizes and had the first combine in the area (below).

Prints showing early mechanized farm machinery are especially important in a rural community. Several such photographs were given to the collection, prompting various questioins: where were these machines made and how did they affect village life and employment? Again, museums within the locality can be of great help with dates, makes and usage.

GLOUCESTER FOLK MUSEUM

A. McHAFFIE, B.A. City Leisure Services Officer
J. F. RHODES, M.A. Director of Museums
C. I. MORRIS, M.A. A.M.A. Curator
99—103 WESTGATE STREET, GLOUCESTER GL1 2PS.
Telephone No. (0452) 26467

Your Ref: CIM/SMS

Our Ref: CIM/SMS

28th June 1988

Miss Pinnell,
Sapperton C. of E. School,
Sapperton,
Nr. CIRENCESTER,
Gloucestershire.

Dear Miss Pinnell,

Thank you for your request for further information on the tractor in the photograph which you left at the F.A. Museum in connection with the Sapperton Photograph Book.

It is a steam tractor. I have no found an illustration of an identical model, but the nearest I have come across is the second International Harvester steam tractor of 1921. Two such prototype steam tractors were produced by the International Harvester Co. of Chicago, Illinois. Both tractors were operated experimentally and were used for ploughing and other field work. However, neither was developed commercially, so it is unlikely that either prototype found its way over to this country.

You mentioned in your note that the people moved to the farm c.1920, so the above date for a similar model that actually went into commercial production would tie in quite well.

I hope that this will help a little. If you want to compare illustrations, the reference is Michael Williams "Steam Power in Agriculture", Blandford, 1977 (Buc. no. 98. It might also be useful to have a look at "The Farm Tractor" by John Appleyard, David & Charles, 1987 although I have not actually seen a copy of this publication.

Meanwhile, I wish you well with your book.

Yours sincerely,

C. I. Morris

Enc.

Ruth

Percy Philpotts

Ruth Philpotts, who died December 1989.

Sidney, Agnes and the Ractliffe family grew older at Beacon Farm and we began to see, from the many photographs which we had been given, that our community was very close-knit in those days. In 1936 Ruth Ractliffe to whom we owe thanks for all these Beacon Farm photographs married Percy Philpotts from Hailey Farm next door. When Sidney and Agnes retired from Beacon Farm they moved along the road to Cowcombe Farm.

Ruth Philpotts and her daughter, Norma, found the sequence of early Ratcliffe family photographs, which had hung relatively unnoticed on their farmhouse walls since being taken.

These are the menfolk of the largest farm in our area. In 1871 Court Farm (now named Manor Farm) employed 24 men and 8 boys. Seated left is Mr. Chamberlain, senior. The other adults are his sons. Centre back is Mr. Freddie Chamberlain who ran the farm and employed Arthur Woolley as his shepherd. The young lad is Douglas, son of Mr. Freddie Chamberlain.

hearing at Beacon Farm c.1930

On these dry top fields sheep were
of prime importance and so was
a good shepherd.

Aptly named Shepherd A. Woolley is
leading Earl Bathurst's flock of 500 ewes and
lambs across the Ten Rides after dipping.

Mrs. Ann Young, his daughter and our
playground supervisor, told us about
shepherd's life. She stressed how
the post of shepherd was not earned
lightly. Mr. Woolley began working
at Court Farm first as a ploughman,
walking miles behind the plough from
dawn till dark. His wife took his
dinner to him in his work field.
It was many years before he
gained the skills necessary to
become a shepherd.

71

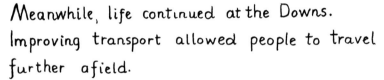

Meanwhile, life continued at the Downs.
Improving transport allowed people to travel
further afield.
In August 1910 the Clark family spent a
holiday in Clovelly and Lynton. Young Elizabeth
and her mother, in matching sun bonnets, are
pictured left experiencing two means of transport.

1910

Florence and her
sisters enjoyed drama
and dressing up.
Here she is as Mrs.
Jarley from "The
Old Curiosity Shop,"
by Charles Dickens.

Proof of ballot card

Yet farming and Chapel work did not fully occupy Charles Clark. He tried three times to capture the vote of electors as their County Councillor for the Bisley Division. He was defeated in 1904 and again in 1907 by only 5 votes (Critchley 628 - Clark 623). Finally, in 1913, he won a majority for the Liberals of 66 (Clark 662 - Aikin-Sneath 596), and a battery of guns was fired to celebrate the victory.

He had long been politically conscious. In 1904 he disagreed with the Education
Act of 1902, which made the County Councils responsible for funding schools, including
Church of England ones which would only employ Church of England teachers.
He disliked the principle of the Act so much that he and his brother Henry, (pictured
right), of nearby Beacon Farm, withheld the portion of their rates that would have
paid for this . . .

Some of Charles Clark's belongings from the Downs Farm were seized and were supposed to be sold in Stroud to pay this debt.

All auctioneers at the Corn Exchange, Stroud, refused to organise the bidding so auctioneers were sent from Gloucester. But by then no potential buyers would bid, so the chairs etc., were put back on the waggon and we can see in the photograph on the left Charles about to triumphantly return home, cheered by his many supporters. (He is raising his hat next to the gentleman wearing the black top hat right of centre.)

When we found this photograph in the Downs collection it made us wonder what jobs were open to most girls when they left school.

What choices were available? It made us search the records to find out.

The boys of Frampton Mansell usually went to work on farms but the proportion of agricultural labourers was much smaller in Sapperton than in Frampton Mansell:-
Frampton Mansell, 58 out of 226 people,
Sapperton, 56 out of 339.
It seemed that more Sappertonians worked in the larger houses or were employed in the woods by Lord Bathurst.

The alternative for girls was domestic service.

For example, Major-General Key had the following household in 1871 in Sapperton:

1. George Key. Maj-Gen.   58
2. Jane   "   Wife   55
3. Emily "   Daughter   23
4. Ann Rogers. Housekeeper 49

5. Louisa Jarman. Ladies Maid. 39
6. Mary Sands. Housemaid. 33
7. Jessie Neil. Kitchenmaid. 22
8. Martha Bishop. Under
    housemaid. 15

9. Robert Rogers, Butler   39
10. John Lingwood. Footman. 18
11. Henry Brown. Coachman.
                            36

It would be with a family like this that most of the girls who went into domestic service would have found employment. This fashionable wedding group was provided by Walter Ractliffe, youngest son of Sidney and Agnes of Beacon Farm. He thinks it was taken around 1902.

On Mothering Sunday we imagined all the servants a rich family would have (left).

Later we went to the Gloucester Folk Museum to see how the maids had to

work in the kitchen of a big house (left).

Above, right, is Bessie Parker who lived near the railway line in Frampton Mansell. Doreen Gardiner, who found the picture, heard from an aunt that Bessie was in service pre-1921 with the Upjohns of "Greencourt" in Chalford, later marrying a Mr. Whiting. Her brother was the local crossing keeper.

On Mothering Sunday we went to church. We acted as a Victorian family would have done. Major General Key was rich and had maids, gardeners and kitchen boys. The maids made little cakes to take home to their mothers on this day half-way through Lent.
The working boys picked small bunches of flowers to take home as well.

David   (10)

We discovered that there was always plenty to do in the dairy for the girls at farms. Left is the butter churn, turning it made arms ache. Centre is the cheese press. All these implements had to be kept meticulously clean.

It meant hours of hard work.

Far right Joanna is straining the curd which will be made into cheese. The whey can be drawn off at the tap.

(We do thank the staff at the Gloucester Folk Museum for their help.)

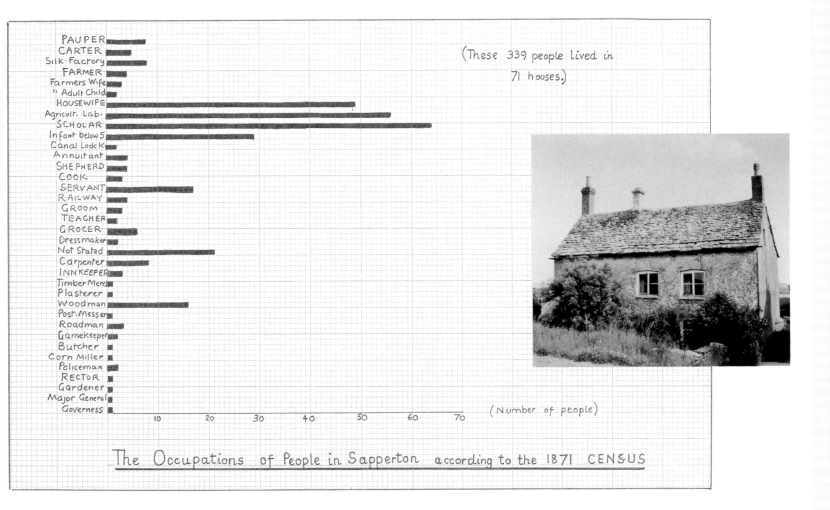

(These 339 people lived in 71 houses.)

PAUPER	
CARTER	
Silk Factory	
FARMER	
Farmers Wife	
" Adult Child	
HOUSEWIFE	
Agricult. Lab.	
SCHOLAR	
Infant below 5	
Canal Lock K	
Annuitant	
SHEPHERD	
COOK	
SERVANT	
RAILWAY	
GROOM	
TEACHER	
GROCER	
Dressmaker	
Not Stated	
Carpenter	
INN KEEPER	
Timber Merch	
Plasterer	
Woodman	
Post. Messer	
Roadman	
Gamekeeper	
Butcher	
Corn Miller	
Policeman	
RECTOR	
Gardener	
Major General	
Governess	

10   20   30   40   50   60   70   (Number of people)

The Occupations of People in Sapperton according to the 1871 CENSUS

Joanne, in our class, was able to look back at her great grandmother and her great, great grandmother, thanks to photographs carefully preserved by her mother, Mrs. Libby Robbins. The close proximity of this family made it easier for us to realise how much life had changed for them in the last hundred years.

1912

Florence Elliott, of the Oak Inn, left our school in 1909. Pictured right is her certificate proving attendance. The earlier picture of haymaking, taken below the Frampton Mansell to Sapperton road, shows Florence's mother, Emily Elliott, standing in the back row, third from the right. It also shows how neighbours, friends and family combined to help in the busy seasons of the farming year.

SCHEDULE III.

Local Education Authority GLOUCESTERSHIRE COUNTY COUNCIL

LABOUR CERTIFICATE, No. 1 (a) (for total exemption after 13 years of age).

AGE AND EMPLOYMENT.	PREVIOUS ATTENDANCE.

I certify that _Florence Elliott_

residing at _(Bailey) Frampton_

was on the _28th_ day of _July_ 19_07_, not

less than **thirteen** years of age, having been born on the _6th_

day of _March_ 1896, as appears by the

Registrar's Certificate [*or the Statutory Declaration*] now produced to

me, and has been shown to the satisfaction of the local education

authority for this district to be beneficially employed.

(Signed) _____

(1) Clerk to the Local Education Authority.

(1) or other officer.

I certify that _Florence Elliott_,

residing at _Frampton_,

has made 350 attendances in not more than two schools during each

year for five preceding years, whether consecutive or not, as shown

by the (2) certificate furnished by the Principal Teacher of the (3)

Oakridge School.

(Signed) _____

(1) Clerk to the Local Education Authority.

(1) or other officer.

(2) For this certificate see Schedule VI.

(3) Here name School or Schools in which the attendances have been made.

Dated the _28th_ day of _July_ 19_07_

N.B.—In districts where the bye-laws extend to the age of fourteen, this Certificate can only be granted if the bye-laws permit full time exemption on an attendance qualification.

4634—A & E. W.—28005/C58—60,000—2·09

We found that we were building a detailed picture of rural life from photographs, census returns, parish records and personal memories. We know from the census that in 1871 there were 8 carpenters working in Sapperton plus a timber merchant and sawmill at Daneway. This picture, discovered in an antique shop, shows the workshop of Richard Harrison around 1900.

Richard Harrison is seated centre with his wife beside him. After the Rector and the farmer at Court Farm he was the most important villager. His wheelwright's workshop was near the Church.

84

Prints turn up in unexpected places. This photograph was given to the infants' teacher, Mrs Shearer, by a friend who found it, quite by chance, in an antique shop.

At one time Richard Harrison employed a dozen men in his carpenter's shop, including his brother John (seated far left), who was an excellent wheelwright.

Richard's high standard of workmanship, providing training for many school-leavers in Sapperton, was one of the reasons for the group known as the Sapperton Craftsmen settling here.

Brother John was also the landlord of the Bell Inn but died before the older Richard.

John's widow Eliza, (pictured right) is described by Norman Jewson in his book, "By Chance I did Rove."

After a few years as landlady of the Bell she retired to a cottage opposite the school. When she was over 80 years old money was scarce so she turned her home into a small general store.

She is still remembered taking her three or four fowls for an airing on the Green which lay at the top of her extremely tidy garden. Stanley Gardiner found us this pre 1900 picture of her.

The Bell Inn c.1900

Here is Eliza in her cottage garden
around 1930. The house overlooks
the area of grass called Grandmothers
Green.
We owe Eliza our thanks for it was
she who handed Miss Jewson's
father the two photographs we
treasure of the village paupers.

The site of the Post Office varies in
our village. We know of four places
it has been housed. In the early 1900s it was opposite the Bell Inn.

The village shop used to be the first house on the right as you enter Church Lane (see map next page). Nora Annesley writes:

"I often visited the shop for my mother and for my father's tobacco. An ounce of "Westward Ho" tobacco cost 4½ old pence. With the change from sixpence I could buy several kinds of sweets; Sherbert Dabs, Liquorice Ladders and Shoe Laces, Allsorts, Humbugs and Hazelnut Creams; one penny purchased quite a few of these.

Richard and John Harrison married Emma and Eliza Chambers whose parents kept the shop and brewed beer."

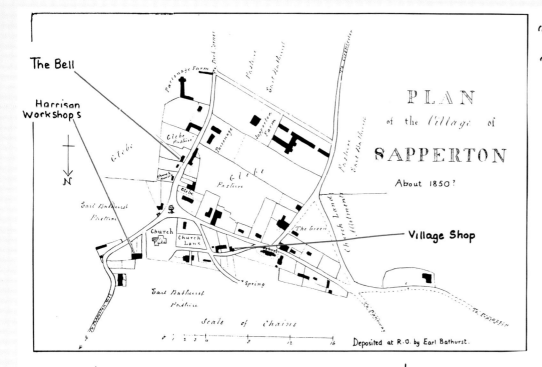

PLAN

of the *village* of

SAPPERTON

About 1850?

The Bell

Harrison Workshops

Village Shop

Scale of Chains

Deposited at R.O. by Earl Bathurst.

"When I was young", explains Nora, "my grandfather Harrison's workshop was a very busy place. Wagons, carts, gates, doors, coffins, they could make anything of wood.

There was a blacksmith's shop on the premises where all kinds of iron work was made. Two horses lived in a stable, Smiler and Kitty, and they were used to transport materials.

Nearby was a saw-pit where large pieces of tree-trunks were sawn into planks. (One man stood at ground level holding one end of a long saw and another less experienced man stood down in the pit and held the other end of the saw. As the two men sawed together all the sawdust fell down on the man underneath.)

These planks were stored in a large shed to dry thoroughly for months. It was a wonderful place for children to play. We were sometimes lent old tools to see how they worked."

As we studied the 1851 and 1871 census returns for our valley we realised how very self-sufficient its inhabitants were. Most people were employed in or near their own village, worked to benefit their immediate locality and used materials which could be found close at hand.

All around Sapperton lay the raw materials needed by the carpenters and wheelwrights (Harrisons and Gardiners), of the village workshops to make their most important product – the wagon.

Oak for the wheel-spokes, elm for the hubs, ash for the shafts and a high quality of workmanship from the craftsmen became their ingredients for success.

Logs near the sawmill at Daneway. 1900-1906

We were able to learn more about these local trades with the help of the Gloucester Folk and Waterways Museums. Here our Sapperton 'workmen' discover the hard work involved as they handle the genuine tools in the museum workshops.

Meanwhile, three other friends were seeking a spiritual home. Ernest Gimson and Ernest and Sidney Barnsley, devotees of William Morris, architects and craftsmen themselves, were searching for somewhere to settle.

To quote their friend Norman Jewson," In the unspoilt country where tradition in the building and surviving crafts, such as the wheelwrights work and blacksmithing still held good, they felt they could find the right setting for a real revival of building and handicrafts, free from the taint of commercialism or deadly monotony of machine production.
So they came to Gloucestershire."

Ernest Barnsley was one of the founder members, with Sidney Barnsley and Ernest Gimson, of the group calling itself the 'Sapperton Craftsmen' which flourished in the valley from 1894 until about 1914. They were determined to keep alive the traditions and standards of English craftsmanship. Examples of their work can be found in many homes around the country and Cheltenham Museum and Art Gallery has a large collection on show.

They believed Pinbury Park, a mile from Sapperton to be an ideal site, magnificently situated overlooking a deeply wooded valley. Its many outbuildings became their workshops in 1894.

Plasterwork (left), chair (centre right) and an inlaid coffer were all in the making in the Pinbury workshop in 1903. We are indebted to our school governor, Miss Nancy Jewson for this and many of the pictures in this section. She is the grand-daughter of Ernest Barnsley.

At Upper Dorvel House
the two daughters of Ernest
Barnsley, Mary (who married
Norman Jewson) and Nelly,
read under a moulded
plaster frieze. c 1910

Ernest Gimson's days
were mainly taken up with
designing for his cabinet-
makers and blacksmiths and
making architectural drawings
but he always managed
to find the time to make
the moulded plasterwork
with his own hands; he
enjoyed it so.

93

ERNEST
GIMSON
1864-1919

As more people came to know of the search for old photographs some were able to send in other valuable old documents as well. Miss Ann Gimson sent this brochure detailing the work of Ernest Gimson.

Pinbury March 17 /95

Dear Sarah, Today is a day for the country. You would rejoice to be at Pinbury in weather like this. A house is an encumbrance. Every hour indoors is an hour wasted. Clothes are almost an encumbrance too. This morning I spent in Franccomb Wood with the dogs. This afternoon Pinbury went to gather watercresses in Dorval wood. We had tea in the garden hatless and waistcoatless. After tea Sid and I strolled to Sapleton and condoled with each other. He that I was a bachelor and I that he was going to be married. When we got back the blackbirds were singing for the first time this year on the tops of the two big elms, and the starlings were gayling on the chimneys. Our snowdrops are in full bloom. The crocuses are promising to be brilliant under the sycamores. The squills are in blossom here and there. And the hepaticas you gave me have produced about a dozen flowers between them. The Crown Imperials are just showing above ground. In the woods the catkins are in their perfections, the palm is in big bud and in sheltered places there is a primrose or two.

We had a hatched chicken yesterday

We are lucky enough to own this original letter sent by Ernest Gimson to his sister Sarah in 1895. It is worth the struggle with the writing!

We hope for another of next week, and the work after that we are expecting some ducklings and goslings.

I am glad Mentor is doing what he can for the Jewry Wall. I heard about it from Thackeray Turner. I should think there is a good chance of saving it as it is not by any means simply local interest.

I am afraid I don't feel very much inclined to meet you and Maggie in London, for one thing I am behind-hand with my work and for another I don't care to leave Pinbury in the Spring any more than is necessary. It is wicked I know, but at present picture exhibitions have no attraction for me, or theatres either. I don't believe I shall ever go to London again of my own free will.

Mrs Blow is coming to stay at the House on April 6. I am hoping she will staying long enough for you to see her. Mr and Mrs G.P. Bankart come to stay with me on May the 4th for a week. I shall probably see them before that time on my way to Scarborough.

Hope to hear better news of Mother soon. This warm weather ought to help her along. Give my love to her please and to everybody else

Yr affectionate brother
Ernest

We were thrilled to be given it by Miss Ann Gimson from Wiltshire two years ago. The writer has such a descriptive style that as you read the letter you are transported to the tranquil life which prevailed at the end of the 19th century.

The three friends and some of their families at Pinbury 1895. Left to right: Sidney Barnsley, Lucy Morley, Ernest Gimson, Alice Barnsley, Ernest Barnsley with his two children, Ethel and Mary.

The small boy on his mother's knee is Edward Barnsley, aged 9 months, son of Sidney and Lucy Barnsley, with his 4 year old sister Grace.

The picture was taken in Nov. 1900 in their garden at Pinbury.

When Edward grew up he took his talents to the Edward Barnsley Workshop at Petersfield, Hants., making hand crafted quality furniture.

Grace followed in the family tradition, making hand painted china, some examples of which were included in Queen Mary's Dolls House, we were informed by the late May Sumsion who used to stay with the family at Pinbury. We are grateful to Edward's widow, Mrs. Tania Barnsley for sharing her family photographs with us.

97

Mrs Gimson née Emily Ann Thompson.

Ernest Gimson was an extremely talented man, excelling in architecture, furniture-design, metal-work and moulded plaster. At the time of writing our letter (1895) he was still a bachelor; however, in 1900, he married the daughter of a Yorkshire rector. She took a great interest in village affairs and paid frequent visits to the school where it is often recorded in the Log Book, "Mrs. Gimson came to play for Country Dancing."

The children pictured right may well have been participants on the Saturday evenings in the Village Hall when the Gimsons and Cecil Sharp revived the villagers interest in old folk songs and country dances.

Pre 1914

Perusing school logbooks and admission registers is particularly profitable to those interested in the history of their local community. They not only give attendance records, they detail the course of each school day, record costs, gifts and visits. Some logbooks can still be found in the schools themselves, but most are in local record offices where their contents are subject to a closure order, which only allows them to be examined once they are fifty years old.

These two items show how Peter Waals, the Dutch foreman
who came from London at the same time as Gimson and the
Barnsleys, liked every piece of furniture he made to be as near
perfect as possible. We really admired the wonderful craftsmanship.

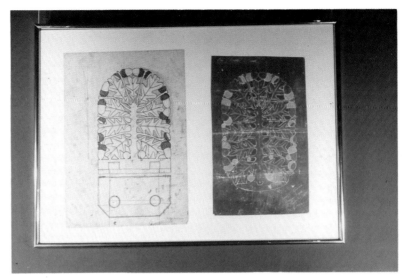

A pair of candle sconces.

Gimson trained Alf Bucknell in the village smithy, making strap hinges and latches. Then he graduated to delicate work in copper, brass and steel, following Gimson's designs. As we can see from the plans (top right) the work involved was very intricate.

Alf Bucknell, a local lad, became a fine blacksmith, carrying on his craft in the neighbourhood for his whole life. His son now does so in nearby Bisley.

John Kimpton, a woodwork master at the Marling School, Stroud, studied the Sapperton Craftsmen for his Dip. Ed. thesis and we are grateful he took all these lovely slides of their work as he traced the whereabouts of each piece in museums, art galleries and local country houses, thus enabling us to share their work and to realise why they still have so many admirers today.

After six years at Pinbury, Lord Bathurst reclaimed it for his own use, but he provided money and land for the three friends to build homes to their own design in the village, namely Beechanger, The Leasowes and Upper Dorvel House.

Mr. Smith (below left), a tenant of Daneway House, vacated it for their use as a workshop and showroom.

c.1880-1890   c.1900

The three friends and their workmen (above right) restored Daneway as they had Pinbury. It was a beautiful old house, built between 1250 and 1300 A.D., continuously inhabited and the home of the Hancox family from 1397 to 1860. Lord Bathurst had recently purchased it.

When Miss Ann Gimson wrote to us, she kindly sent us several copies of these book-plates (below) which Ernest Gimson designed for his brother Sidney.

The middle picture shows his house "The Leasowes" before the thatch burned and was replaced with tiles. Right shows a good example of a perfectly proportioned Gimson rocking chair.

This is Beechanger not very long after it was designed and built
by Sidney Barnsley 1902-3. It must have been wonderful for
him to be given the land and money to test out his first design
in the domestic housing field knowing it was to be his own.

Jan 1905

The simple clean lines of the interior of Beechanger epitomise all the group valued. "It was a completely new style ... in its design, grace of form was combined with extreme simplicity to emphasise the beauty ..." wrote Norman Jewson in his book "By chance I did rove."

Ernest Gimson hoped to start a craft village near Sapperton where people with similar values to himself and his two friends could live in great happiness, producing beautiful things by hand. He hated all machinery and would not even allow a circular saw in his workshops.

He and his friends, working with the Sapperton masons, carpenters, wheelwrights and blacksmiths, built a memorable reputation which still causes followers to regularly visit our village ninety years later.

His dream did not materialise, for in 1914 the Great War halted the world. Afterwards, the simple country ways which the Craftsmen had so respected, changed and had gone forever. The young men who were lucky enough to return had been through such a period of change and devastation that they often did not wish to return to the old ways.

Then, in 1919 Ernest Gimson died and the whole idea was abandoned. The Daneway workshop closed and Daneway House had various tenants.

One of these was Oliver Hill, an artist. The pictures on the opposite page are from around his time, thirty years later.

(Pictures from Architecture Illustrated, Dec. 1949. Printed by Arthurs Press, Ltd., Woodchester. Edited by H.W. Morton-Kaye and drawn to our attention by our friend Stanley Gardiner of France Lynch).

DANEWAY HOUSE 1949

107

In 1914
there began
a conflict which
was to be called "the
war to end all wars."

THE GREAT WAR 1914-1918

8,634,000 lives were lost and
our menfolk were
scattered across the
globe.

Victor Harrison, brother of
Nora Annesley, was killed, age 23
and buried in France.

Harry Walker
returned safely.

So did Reg Gobey.

We found out about the war as many people sent us photographs of men in
uniform. Who were these young men? Which ones survived? As the war dragged on
many thousands were killed. By 1916 there was a shortage of soldiers so a law
was passed saying all fit men must go to fight. For our young men, leaving the
peace of our area for the hell of the trenches in France must have been almost unbearable.

Reg Gobey 1920   Fred Whiting (seated)   Sybil Whiting & Gordon Harrison

The war had a profound effect on those involved. The young men of this valley
travelled far. Reg Gobey, our school cook's father, found himself in the Middle East,
while the sailors Fred Whiting and Gordon Harrison circled the globe. On their return
they married local girls, Reg settling down at Pinbury with Etheldrida Whiting
and Gordon, Nora's other brother, married Etheldrida's sister Sybil and made
their home at Puck Mill. Fred Whiting married Bessie Parker of Frampton Mansell.

Percy Philpotts 1918   Did this unamed Aussie ever get back home, we wondered?

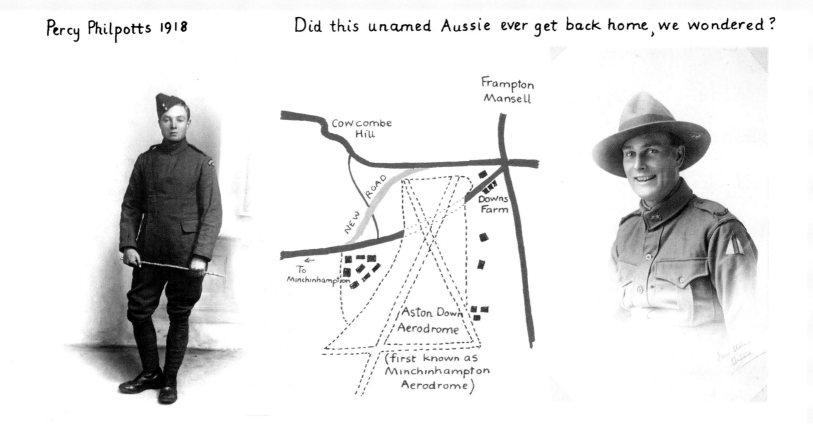

Percy Philpotts joined the newly formed Royal Flying Corps. This was the first war to use aeroplanes. The road from the Downs to Minchinhampton was re-routed to allow a new airfield to be developed in 1918. The Australians trained here and nearby Leighterton and 24 died here. Of course, some of the young Australians called at nearby homes, the one right, left his photo at The Downs!

The war also had its effect on the women who stayed behind, opening up unforeseen opportunities; for many it provided their first paid jobs outside the home.

Florrie Clark did Red Cross work then trained as a midwife. Her sister Eva completed her medical training and went to Delhi to be a doctor in a Mission Hospital there. The right-hand picture shows Florrie with Peter, the first of three babies she would adopt and bring up as her own.

After the war the villagers grieved for those who did not return. But life went on and the rhythm of essential tasks helped them to overcome sorrow. Haymaking will not wait. Jack Musty (left) found his horse useful for hay-raking on the steep Frampton fields, as did Bill Roberts, Samuel Ash and Arthur Roberts (below). Far left are some of the Ractliffe boys with a hay-making gang at Beacon Farm.

Pictures by courtesy of Mrs. Musty.

In Memoriam.

Dr. EVA MARY CLARK,
DELHI.
July 11th, 1922.

Dennis Moss & Peckham,   Stroud.

The whole locality had been so proud of Eva that her early death
in India from typhoid came as a further blow (1922). Under the
leadership of Charles Clark, the Baptists of Frampton Mansell decided
that a fitting War Memorial would be a Chapel, which would honour Eva, too.
In 1924 its Foundation Stone was laid by Maj-Gen. Sir Fabian Ware (War Graves Commission).

Eva was much missed by her Bible Class which met at the Downs Farm each week.

Ten young men lost their lives in the War and so many deaths stunned the community and life never regained its pre-war rhythm. In later years Mrs. Clark used the Bath Chair seen right, being propelled by Florrie. They often came down to the village of Frampton Mansell, visiting and helping the elderly there. Lower right we see the village shop, run by Mr. & Mrs. Stayte, great grandparents of Joanne Robbins in our class. Mrs. Paine, who lived next door, is standing at the back wearing a typical large black hat.

Mindy is also in our class and she too can trace her family through many of the photographs.

We met Mr. Samuel Ash earlier, one of Mindy's great-grandfathers, and here another, Mr. Jones, is guiding the bull at Cowcombe Farm.

This farm was where Sidney and Agnes Ractliffe spent their retirement when they left the larger Beacon Farm.

Left we see Gerald Whiting, brother of Sybil, Dorothy and Etheldrida, all of Tunnel mouth Cottage. Born in 1900, he missed the fighting but went to Germany with the Army just after 1918. This gave him a love of motors which led him to spend most of his life as a chauffeur. In this 1922 photograph, taken in Drew's builders yard at nearby Chalford, he is seated nearest to the camera.

Every village has its share of
"characters" and stories abound
concerning their exploits.

We were told these three ladies above,
Mrs. Bidmead, Mrs. Rose Phelps (centre) and
Mrs. Fred. Parker (right) had noticed a tree
in the centre of Frampton which was in a dangerous condition. They were
told that they could have it if they could get it felled.

Not to be beaten they approached Jesse Miller who lived rough in the
nearby Cowcombe Woods. He willingly obliged and the gleeful ladies
then sawed the fallen tree into logs themselves.

As life-long Sappertonians Lewis and Hilda Allen have a store of memories which they have willingly shared with us. Although life has changed in many ways - some of them dramatic - since the advent of the camera, others too were able to tell us of a custom which has survived to the present day.

Until well after the Second World War the ladies of the village would set out together, usually on a Thursday afternoon, to go "wooding" in the bottom of the valley. They collected logs and fallen branches and returned loaded with their 'burdens' of fuel for the coming week.

One stalwart lady prided herself on being able to cope with two 'burdens'.

It is still a common sight to see the older villagers setting out "wooding," although they now use 'modern' wheeled transport to help them in their task.

Here we see Lewis and Hilda with their wooding truck.

Sadly Lewis died in December 1989.

This project – this photographic history – was a very "on-going" exercise. The more we hunted, the more old pictures we found, and the more memories we stirred.

Some of our finds were on our doorstep. Pictures taken at the turn of the century can still be found lying in attics, in old albums and in some cases hanging on walls where they have been for generations since being taken.

Others have travelled hundreds of miles as their owners moved away from the village and were returned to us by train, car and post.

We did not know what lucky finds awaited us each new day. A map showing the source of each photograph would indicate how far a once tightly-knit community has been scattered, but each owner had fond memories of Sapperton.

Some were discovered quite by chance. The project was mentioned to one teacher living miles away and the name "Jessie Carrington" cropped up.

"How strange," she said, "My mother lived in Chalford, and Jessie Carrington was her best friend. I'm sure I have some pictures of them together. I'll have a little search!"

And so the picture of the three bathing belles at Weston-super-Mare joined our collection...

As our collection of old photographs grew we were amazed at the interest shown in it locally.

Slowly we realised that this interest was shared by a great many people who had a love of their environment. They all enjoyed going back into the past. We realised the pleasure we had obtained from our collection should be shared with others. Maybe we could even influence them to collect a set of pictures of their own neighbourhood as a visual historical record.

We recalled seeing H.R.H. The Duke of York on T.V. looking at old photographs of his family with an archivist at Windsor and knew this joy of delving into our past was shared by many, regardless of rank.

Publication of our collection seemed a good way of sharing our pleasure and a possible means of encouraging a wider awareness of the value of these irreplaceable old sepia-coloured photographs.

The children found calling on people within the community often produced marvellous 'finds' from long overdue searches of attics.

120

As we reached the conclusion of our project we felt that we had achieved our aim and knew our village and its recent history better.
We could look at nearly every cottage, house and farm and accurately imagine the family who lived there 70 to 100 years ago.
We had brought our neighbourhood, its history and its inhabitants to life.

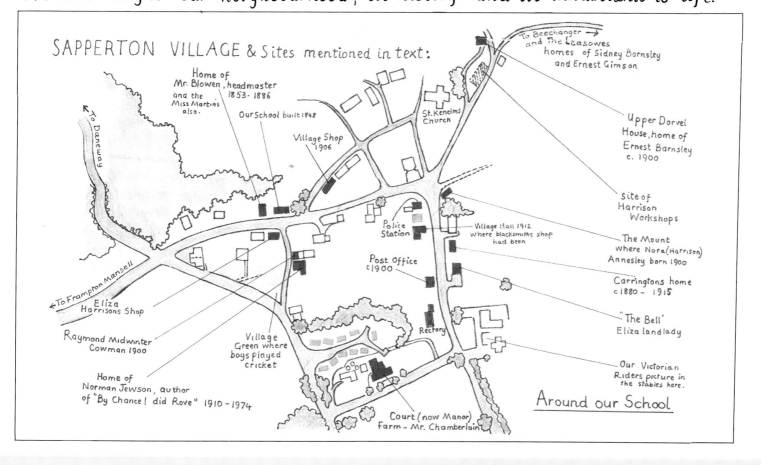

SAPPERTON VILLAGE & Sites mentioned in text:

To Daneway

To Frampton Mansell

Home of Mr. Blowen, headmaster 1853-1886 and the Miss Martins also.

Our School built 1848

Village Shop 1906

St. Kenelms Church

To Beechanger → and The Leasowes homes of Sidney Barnsley and Ernest Gimson

Upper Dorvel House, home of Ernest Barnsley c. 1900

Site of Harrison Workshops

Police Station

Village Hall 1912 where blacksmiths shop had been

The Mount where Nora (Harrison) Annesley born 1900

Post Office c1900

Carringtons home c 1880 - 1915

Eliza Harrisons Shop

Raymond Midwinter Cowman 1900

Village Green where boys played cricket

Home of Norman Jewson, author of "By Chance I did Rove" 1910-1974

Rectory

"The Bell" Eliza landlady

Our Victorian Riders picture in the stables here.

Around our School

Court (now Manor) Farm - Mr. Chamberlain

121

We discovered farmers, wheelwrights teachers, maids and children as they all trooped before the camera lens.

Rich men, poor men,

Beggar men... but no thieves!

Looking back through our collection it is obvious that we like PEOPLE. We feel that the Village is like a living body. The houses, solid, unbending and long-lasting, resemble the boney skeleton.

But it is the PEOPLE who populate the village that are its heart, and their job of work, their employment, is the life-blood that keeps the village sound and healthy.

We had many views and street scenes offered to us for our collection but our love of PEOPLE guided our choice so we usually selected scenes with human interest as well.

The trickle of photographs which aroused our interest in the beginning never turned into a flood but they gave us clues, providing a starting point from which we gently and politely probed and questioned likely donors, advertised by parish magazine and pulpit and researched local records.

Likely donors — ah! who are they?

Likely donors are usually people who have not moved house too many times, for each house-move heralds a clear out- the death knell to old photographs and memorabilia.

We find naturally the older generations have the most to tell us but often sympathetic off-spring can prod failing memories, with splendid results.

It has all been such fun.

It has all been so satisfying to find a rare gem, a lost scene, that we urge everyone who reads this to have a go... ... save the past for the future.

They say you plant a walnut tree for your heirs and lay down a cellar of fine wines for your children's children. So it should be with photographs depicting social change.

Schools as small as ours may be rare in future so we intend to leave behind a pictorial record of the last few years, placed in safekeeping for future historians.

We wonder what people of the 21st century will think of us?

Regional newspapers and parish magazines are worthwhile points from which to advertise. The newspapers themselves have extensive archives which can be tapped for relevant items.

A photograph of Sapperton C.E. School taken by "The Photographer," Gloucester, March 1990

The quality of any publication would depend on our finding sponsors prepared to support us. We approached the Country Landowners Educational Trust and were thrilled at their enthusiastic response, and as our major sponsors we owe them our deepest thanks. Knowing their interest in the countryside we asked Shell U.K. and Coca-Cola for their help too. We are extremely grateful to both for their essential aid. To all our good friends who shared their family treasures with us we give our heartfelt thanks and hope they will feel this book a worthy memorial.